Table of Contents

BUILDING THE FOUNDATION 11

WHY THE RAPID INDUCTION FORMULA? 29

WHAT'S ALL THE FUSS ABOUT? 32

RAPID OR INSTANT? 35

THE RAPID BENEFIT 37

AVOID THE TRAP 41

HYPNOTIC EXPERIENCES & EXERCISES 45

THE NUTS AND BOLTS 57

THE GLUE THAT BRINGS IT TOGETHER 72

GET THEM DEEPER 83

WAKEY, WAKEY! 92

RAPID RE-INDUCTIONS 99

YOUR QUESTIONS ANSWERED! 102

NOW YOU KNOW! 117

Dan Candell's Rapid Induction Formula

HOW TO HYPNOTIZE ANYONE
QUICKLY

Insider Secrets of A Real Hypnotist: Dan Candell

Dan Candell Hypnosis, LLC.

NORTHBOROUGH, MA.Copyright © 2019 by Dan Candell.

All rights reserved. No part of this publication may be reproduced, distributed or transmitted in any form or by any means, including photocopying, recording, or other electronic or mechanical methods, without the prior written permission of the publisher, except in the case of brief quotations embodied in critical reviews and certain other non-commercial uses permitted by copyright law. For permission requests, email Dan Candell at the email address below.

Dan Candell Hypnosis, LLC.

www.RapidInductionFormula.com

www.DanCandell.com

email: dancandell@gmail.com

The Rapid Induction Formula. Dan Candell. —1st ed.

Content Editing: Byron Paul Hynes

ISBN 978-1-7326460-2-5

Special Bonus For Reading This Book!

Along with this book, you also get a free mini-course that has examples and additional video instruction. For access to the mini-course, please visit the website below right now!

www.RapidInductionFormula.com/Resources

What Others Are Saying About This Book

Dan Candell's "Rapid Induction Formula" is a MUST HAVE TOOL for every hypnotist, stage or clinical. In this book he clearly outlines the process, dispels any negative thoughts about rapid inductions and teaches this formula in a very succinct and systematic way. This is something you will want to include in your stage show, clinical practice or even hypnotic demonstrations that you may perform, and after reading this book, you will be able to, instantly!!!
- **Michael C. DeSchalit, CHt, CH, CI**

As someone who has created products and programs about rapid inductions, it is clear that Dan has created a new spin on how to do them. His formula for doing rapid and instant inductions goes far beyond a script, it is an easy to follow process that will help the reader create their own inductions as well. This can easily be applied to stage hypnosis, street hypnosis, demonstrational hypnosis, and can also be used with clinical hypnosis. This is a must read for any hypnotist! – **Dr. Richard K. Nongard, LMFT – President of ICBCH**

As creator of NFNLP and author of several books, I have been doing this for longer than Dan has been alive. It is great to see that he can breathe life back into something that has been around for centuries. Dan breaks the rapid induction process down so anyone can not only do it, but also understand it. The Rapid Induction Formula is a perfect description and title for the book as much like NLP, it's about the process and not just about the script. He also adds a lot of subtleties to the process to make even more effective for the hypnotist.
- **Dr. William D. Horton, Psy.D, CADC, CI, MH – Author of Habits For Success**

Foreword

For the last few years, whenever Dan Candell is introduced, people are often surprised that he's been working with hypnosis for more than half his life (and yes, he started when he was about 12)! In comparison, I've been practicing *longer* than Dan's entire life... and as his beard starts to gray, I may admit to that less often, but it gives us a good point to play on when we're teaching together or speakers at the same event. It's probably those years of head-start that put me in the honored position of being Dan's mentor and business coach, and I'm proud to say he's also a student, colleague and friend. Despite the difference in years, we share a lot of similarities in our experience and how we approach this profession.

Before taking any formal training, I learned at the side of my mentor while he was working with large groups (hundreds of participants), corporate gigs, doing TV talk shows and radio (on a regular circuit), private practice, writing, speaking, and stage hypnosis. This became my standard of what a hypnosis practice was supposed to be. After my initial certification, I went on to take courses from many of the other 'greats', was fortunate to earn a doctoral degree in hypnosis when there was one available, and began immediately giving back to my profession as an instructor, innovator and mentor.

Part of what Dan and I have in common is that we are always learning, and we both look for patterns and create systems. That's really how Dan came into my focus, when he was taking my HypnoCoach® Certification course, I mentioned that I take on a few people for private mentoring, and he immediately applied. I suspect that he recognized the detail, structure and system that he was learning in my trademarked signature course, and knew we were kindred spirits.

Dan's Rapid Induction Formula is just what it sounds like. It's a pattern. It's a system. It's a formula for your success with efficient, effective ways to hypnotize anyone, anywhere, quickly! I learned to do rapid inductions in the beginning of my career because that's what my mentor did... that's how you do a quick demo on TV or in front of a large gathering, and it's also how you can have more efficient private sessions. Both Dan and I have hypnotized people on airplanes, in elevators (or in front of them) and in all kinds of other situations when hypnotizing someone "fast" is necessary or preferred. Dan uses rapid inductions all day, every day in his multi-faceted career. When he's doing stage shows, he keeps a rapid pace and keeps the fun flowing – he's known for being "fast and funny". As a speaker he can do a quick demo with a few people brought to the front, or by going out into the audience. And in his office, he sees more clients in a day than some hypnotists do in a week. Rapid inductions are an important component to Dan's success.

There are many hypnotists who are concerned that they don't know the best way, or the right way to do rapid inductions, or they're afraid that they'll mess it up... and as a result, they often don't even try. In this book, Dan is giving you his secret combination to unlock the power of rapid inductions. Once you know the basic combination and you know how and why it works, then you can practice, and prove to yourself that it works! This is a powerful pattern that Dan is sharing with you.

When I started studying hypnosis all those years ago, I was fascinated by any old hypnosis books I could find, and I began to collect vintage hypnosis materials. All the "old stuff" even from the 1800's still works, and much can be learned from the old methods. I still look for old books and also buy new hypnosis books all the time. I've always been impressed with some of the books that might be smaller or thinner than others, but they get right to the point and give actionable information, that you can immediately start to use. In Dan's new book, you'll find no fluff, and a follow-me formula. Everything Dan has included in this book is aimed at helping you become proficient and more comfortable in using rapid inductions.

If you're just starting out with hypnosis or rapid induction methods, this is a great place to start. And if you're a seasoned pro who's been doing this for years, you might be interested in learning how Dan has deciphered the process into a useful formula, to help you create new rapid inductions to add to your repertoire.

Here's my recommended formula: Read the book + follow the formula + practice rapid inductions = impress yourself and others!
- **Dr. Lisa Halpin, DCH, BCH, CI, OB**

CHAPTER 1

Building The Foundation

Congratulations! You have, in the pages of this book, my hypnotic secrets to hypnotize people fast. Now, with great power comes great responsibility. I trust you will use the techniques in this book in an ethical manner.

Initially, I wrote this book as a skill-building book for existing hypnotists, however, the more the word spread, the more I realized that people who see my shows, my videos, attend my seminars, etc. also want to learn these skills. Because of that realization, this chapter is filled with "must know" information. In order to effectively utilize the methods and techniques in this book, you must have a core understanding of hypnosis and how it works. You MUST be able to talk intelligently about hypnosis and explain it to other people. After all, you will be seen as "THE HYPNOTIST."

Within this chapter, you will learn the core competencies of hypnosis and what you must know before using my signature Rapid Induction Formula. Buckle your seatbelt; you're in for a fascinating ride.

Safety First

If you have no experience in hypnosis, I recommend taking (at least) an intro course. Some good organizations to look into that offer certification programs are the National Guild of Hypnotist and also the ICBCH. I am an instructor through both organizations, and either one can provide a great foundation to expand your knowledge even further.

Be Aware

I believe anyone can be hypnotized to some degree, that does not mean that we *should* hypnotize *everyone*. There are some conditions that you want to be aware of to ensure

Dan Candell's Rapid Induction Formula

both you and the subjects that you are hypnotizing stay safe.

Stay away from hypnotizing anyone who is under the influence of drugs and alcohol. Their judgment is already impaired, and their ability to follow instructions will be muted, which can result in a sticky situation (literally and figuratively, I have seen some drunks hypnotized in a stage show vomit all over the stage.)

You also want to avoid hypnotizing people who have epilepsy, mental conditions, severe medical conditions, or injuries. Hypnosis cannot cause medical or psychological problems, but if there is one pre-existing, it can expose it or bring it to light. The last thing you want is for a person to just happen to have a seizure and blame it on hypnosis.

Unless you are working specifically on pregnancy issues or birthing, I would also stay away from hypnotizing pregnant women, especially in public demonstrations. If a pregnant woman fell during your demonstration or stage show, it could do harm to both her and the unborn child.

Basically, use common sense. It will pay off in the long run!

NOTE: I was performing at a high school, and before I went on stage to start the show, the school principal approached me and pointed out a group of students in the audience who were all clustered together. The principal told me, "Dan, those are the stoners, and I don't think they should be in the show because they may cause a problem. Can you say something without directly addressing them?" So, last minute, I started thinking about how I can make this lighthearted. Before I asked for volunteers, I said, "Here are my requirements to volunteer for the show..." I went through my basic requests, and then said, "also, please stay in the audience if you're under any other influence other than being high on life... sound good?" and it got a big laugh. So, that has stuck in my show since then!

Talk The Talk

As I said previously, you need to be able to have an intelligent conversation about hypnosis. One of the best ways to instill confidence in the people you are going to hypnotize is to sound like you know what you're talking about. Here are some common myths and misconceptions that usually come up when talking to people about hypnosis. It will also provide you with a foundational knowledge and perhaps answer some questions you may have about hypnosis. When discussing these things, keep it simple, short, and sweet. Remember, the key to rapid inductions is working fast. If you're having a 20-minute conversation with a person on the street before you hypnotize them, it defeats the purpose. However, some office clients or people attending demonstrations may require you to talk more elaborately about hypnosis.

When I am hypnotized, will I be asleep or unconscious?

No. When you are hypnotized, you won't be asleep or unconscious. You will hear everything that I say, and you'll be totally aware of what's going on. You'll just be so relaxed that you really won't care about anything.

Can I get stuck in hypnosis?

No. If something happened to me while you were hypnotized, you would be totally aware and be able to open your eyes. You are in control the entire time.

Will you be controlling me? I've heard hypnosis is mind control.

No. Hypnosis is not mind control. When you are hypnotized, you will still be in control; you will be in a more receptive state and feel confident in your ability to follow my instructions. You will be and will feel safe at all times. Hypnosis is often used to help people take control over parts of their life that they feel are out of or beyond their control.

What does hypnosis feel like?

Hypnosis is unique for everyone; it's a very subjective experience. Some people feel heavy and relaxed, and other people feel light and floaty. You will hear as much and remember as much as you would from any typical conversation. Your mind will be focused on my voice and on what I instruct you to do. You'll know what's happening, you just won't really care, and you may feel like you're zoning out. It's basically like you will be in a land of "I don't care!"

Can only weak-willed or gullible people be hypnotized? Or can everyone be hypnotized?

Everyone can be hypnotized to some degree, in fact, those people who are more intelligent are usually easier to hypnotize.

What should I do to get hypnotized?

Often, people try too hard. Just follow my simple instructions and suggestions. Don't try to get hypnotized, don't fight against it, instead, let it happen by following every instruction I give you, and it will happen.

What if it doesn't work for me?

Then we move onto a different method that will work for you. However, this method works for most of the people most of the time.

Will I divulge secrets when I am hypnotized? I am afraid of what I will say!

You will NOT divulge secrets or any personal information that you don't want other people to know. You'll be completely aware, and if there is something you don't want to say, you won't say it.

Is Hypnosis Dangerous?

Not inherently, no. It can become dangerous in the hands of an inexperienced person. It can also be dangerous if a hypnotist is practicing out of their scope of practice or hypnotizing someone they should *not* be hypnotizing. Also, if practiced unethically, it can become dangerous. It's just like anything; in the wrong hands, even a child's toy can be dangerous.

A metaphor I like to use is this (a friend of mine gave me this metaphor and it fits perfectly here.) Hypnosis is like a book of matches. A match can be used to produce fire, which can be both a wonderful and dangerous tool. Fire can produce heat, light, and assist in creating food and nourishment. However, in the wrong hands, fire can be used to ignite homes, ruin lives, and even for mass destruction. Hypnosis is a tool that can be used for great and amazing things. However, in the wrong hands, it can be damaging.

Does a hypnotist have special powers?

Powers? No. Knowledge and skill? Yes. Anyone can learn how to hypnotize; however, it is a skill that is developed after practice and experience.

What is hypnosis?

Hypnosis is just a receptive state. It's when we bypass the conscious analytical mind with a hypnotic induction, hypnotic language, or other hypnotic techniques. This gets you into a more agreeable state so that everything I am saying gets to your subconscious mind.

Conscious Mind

The conscious mind is the very logical and analytical part of the mind. That is the part of the mind that is very "surface level" where you analyze everything that is happening. If you're trying to change a behavior or habit, we need to bypass the conscious analytical mind. This is why we use hypnosis.

Subconscious Mind

The subconscious mind is the part of your mind that stores all of your experiences and perceptions. Based on your perceptions, it forms your reality. This is also the part of your mind that stores your habits, feelings, sensations, emotions, personality, and internal programs. This is the part that we communicate with when we use hypnosis.

With hypnosis, we can influence your thoughts, feelings, sensations, emotions, and thus influence your perceptions and concept of reality. That's where we really have fun with hypnosis and can use it as a tool to change lives!

Signs of Hypnosis

Hypnosis can be unique for each individual. However, there are many signs that a person may experience when they are hypnotized. Below, we will go over the subjective and objective indications of hypnosis.

Subjective

These are the signs that the person may notice when they are hypnotized. It is wise to go over these with the person after they were hypnotized, so they know what they experienced was, in fact hypnosis.

Time Distortion: Quite often, when a person is hypnotized, they will feel as if the concept of time disappears. As a result of this, they will usually feel like 20-minutes goes by in only two or three minutes. Sometimes it can also be on the longer end as well. Here are some typical responses:

Client: "It felt like you were only talking to me for about two or three minutes!"

Hypnotist: "I was actually talking to you for about 25 minutes. You experienced time distortion, which is one of the key indicators that you were hypnotized!"

They will also sometimes respond like this...

Client: "It felt like you were talking to me for like three hours!"

Hypnotist: "I was actually only talking to you for about 20 minutes. You've experienced the longer end of time distortion, which is a key indicator that you were hypnotized!"

However, if the client does not experience time distortion, it does not mean that they were not hypnotized, it just means that they did not experience that sign. That may sound like this:

Client: "It felt like you were talking to me for about 24 or 25 minutes..."

Hypnotist: "Yes, you're right. That's great; you were able to stay aware to the point where you know almost exactly the amount of time that I was talking to you. See, I told you that you would still be aware!"

Suggested Amnesia: At the end of most comedy hypnosis shows, I like to suggest amnesia, but then provide a trigger for memories to come back at a later time (usually when they leave the venue or when their friends say a keyword after the show). However, I always suggest that when they do remember, they will remember everything as being a really positive experience. At the end of a session, I will usually suggest that they will remember as much or as little about what I said in the session for them to be successful. Some people will remember bits and pieces, and some people will remember everything, whereas others will remember nothing.

Dan Candell's Rapid Induction Formula

NOTE: Sometimes, if people don't remember, they may be a little disturbed that a part of their memory just vanished. You can re-hypnotize them to remember what happened, but sometimes they still won't remember even when prompted. So, I explain to them that it's almost like a puzzle. They may remember bits and pieces, and they may not, but little memories may come back as they fall asleep. You are seeding that suggestion that they may remember later.

Some other signs they may experience may include heaviness, relaxation, a sense of detachment, or a feeling of floating. They may also notice that they feel a warmth or a coolness, swallowing differently or even seeing colors, shapes, or patterns under their closed eyelids.

You want to go through some of these signs so that you can *verify in their mind* that they were hypnotized. After you get their subjective experience, you can suggest (if they are a client who is coming back for a future session), that they will experience those same signs the next time they re-enter hypnosis.

Objective

When you hypnotize a person, you need to know that they are hypnotized. Here are some things to be aware of and look for…

You may notice that their body and limbs are heavy. If they are standing or sitting in a straight back chair, you may notice them slumped over or their head drooping. You may also notice that their face and jaw are droopy and relaxed. You may also see that they are blush or their facial color changes. Their breathing becomes more regular, and their eyes may flutter. The fluttering of the eyelids is called REM, or Rapid Eye Movement. This usually happens when we are in REM or dream sleep, and it can increase in the client if they are visualizing something.

You want to observe these signs and take a mental note so you can tell the client or subject(s) how you know they were hypnotized.

NOTE: If you hypnotize a person and you are not going to do any "hypnotic phenomena," and just give them positive suggestions, it's crucial that you notice the objective signs and ask them what they experienced so you can validate hypnosis for them. I was at a hypnosis convention, and there was a person who was doing rapid inductions on people but did not produce any hypnotic phenomenon. He "hypnotized" about 50 people that day, about 85 percent of them would walk by my table where I was stationed once they were finished with him, and I would hear them saying, "Jeeze, I don't think I was really hypnotized..." This is the last thing you want people saying. He could have avoided that whole thing by simply validating hypnosis for the person after hypnotized them.

Abreactions

Abreactions are rare. Because I do so many shows, I have had a few abreactions in my shows. There is not really anything you can do to avoid it. Just because they are rare does not mean you don't need to know about them.

The first abreaction I ever encountered was at a post-prom party at 3:00 in the morning. An 18-year-old girl who was hypnotized was participating in the show. About halfway through the show, she started to shake, she was breathing heavy and started to cry.

When I was first trained as a hypnotist back in 2003, the way I was taught to deal with an abreaction was to grab their head, stroke their temples, and whisper sweet nothings in their ear... Don't do this.

Instead, I followed the advice of the late, great Gerald Kein and said, "The scene fades and attend to your breathing." I repeated that until she was calm. I brought her out of hypnosis and said, "I will just have you enjoy the rest of the show from the audience, and you will be immune from hypnosis for the rest of the night. You will stay out of hypnosis for the rest of the night."

Sometimes, if it is a stage hypnosis show setting, it may be wise to have the person leave the room and get some water just to disassociate from the situation.

What is an abreaction? An abreaction is usually an emotional or physical outburst that is unexpected while a person is in hypnosis. People can experience an abreaction for a variety of reasons it's because they have some pent-emotions, and they feel safe to release emotions when they are in hypnosis. It can also be caused by a spontaneous memory of a traumatic event.

I haven't had many people go into abreactions, but every case I have seen, it was usually a female who had a traumatic event happen earlier in their life or something that that they have not processed emotionally yet, such as a breakup or a death in the family. I have also talked to many other hypnotists where the common themes that cause an abreaction are stress and exhaustion.

The major signs of an abreaction are inappropriate or spontaneous crying, laughing, shaking, screaming or moaning, thrashing or emotional outbursts.

When dealing with an abreaction, remember these eight words, "***the scene fades, and attend to your breathing***." Once they are calm, emerge them from hypnosis, tell them that they will stay out of hypnosis for the rest of the night, and excuse them or remove them from the situation.

Unleash The Beast

Now that you have a foundational knowledge about hypnosis, let's talk about how to boost your confidence and your success rate.

Context is everything. If you just went up to a random person, snapped your fingers in front of their face and said, "SLEEP!" You're asking to get smacked...

Embrace the identity of being **THE HYPNOTIST**. You are a hypnotist, and you do rapid hypnosis. Period. That's a real conversation starter.

Just imagine if a random stranger went up to you on the street and started rubbing you all over, that would be weird. However, if that same stranger had a massage chair and a sign that said, "free massages today," you'd jump at the change to get a rubdown!

Be firm, be confident, and be assertive. When you are, it will cause other people to have confidence in you, and it will also increase confidence in yourself. Let's do this!

CHAPTER 2

Why The Rapid Induction Formula?

When you hear the phrase "instant induction," what's the first thing that comes to mind? Do you immediately think of stage hypnosis or a hypnotist performing on the street? Do you think of a person being "slammed" or "pulled" into hypnosis? Do you think of some overly dramatized, forceful method of inducing hypnosis? Non-hypnotists have misconceptions about hypnosis, and I find that in the same way, many hypnotists also have misconceptions about rapid and instant inductions.

When I started doing hypnosis, my interest was in stage hypnosis. I'm "that guy" who started when I was 12. I was trained in stage hypnosis at the age of 14. I soon realized that I didn't like the typical, slower style of hypnosis, such as progressive muscle relaxations (PMR) and other long, drawn-out processes. So, I started exploring various styles of rapid and instant inductions and began tightening up my process. At first, I used these inductions on stage in my hypnosis shows. Then, when I started working with clients, I realized that I could modify these inductions and use them with my clients. My philosophy was, and still is, *why take 10, 20 or even 30-minutes to do something that you can do more effectively and efficiently in one, two, or three minutes?*

I also realized that most rapid and instant inductions were forceful, commanding, and often a shock to the client, volunteer or subject. This didn't sit too well with me. I wondered—as you may have as well—if there was a different way that would get the same results without "slamming" a person into hypnosis.

After years of experimentation and implementation, I finally narrowed it down to a science that I call, "Dan Candell's Signature Rapid Induction Formula," or RIF for short.

The misconceptions about rapid and instant inductions that I hear from hypnotists—or even lay people—include:

- Rapid inductions are too forceful.

- Rapid inductions are only for the stage.

- Rapid inductions are too dramatic.

I am writing this book to clear up those misconceptions, and also to provide an understanding of how every hypnotist can effectively use rapid and instant inductions. My goal is to help all hypnotists feel comfortable with using rapid inductions effectively and efficiently, without any fear.

I am excited to share my knowledge and methodology with you! This book will help accelerate your confidence and increase your capability to hypnotize anyone, anywhere.

**HAPPY HYPNOTIZING
AND ENJOY!**

CHAPTER 3

What's All The Fuss About?

The Rapid Induction Formula (RIF) is a strategic way to induce hypnosis quickly.

You can mix and match different parts of the RIF to create several different inductions. I developed this formula over several years of trial and error, beginning in my stage hypnosis shows. Then, I started applying it to street hypnosis. As it morphed, I then started using in with my private clients.

Most quick inductions are based on the element of surprise, even shocking the nervous system. The premise is often to abruptly surprise the client by shouting "sleep" with an arm pull or even a sudden jerk forward. I used to practice these methods, and the results were sometimes outstanding and sometimes lackluster. These methods often look violent and forceful and can sometimes be disturbing to the client or even to the people watching.

The rapid induction formula takes the opposite approach—no surprise at all. It is based on telling the client what will happen, and establishing four key requirements that will induce hypnosis in the client:

1) Expectation
2) Motivation
3) Belief
4) Willingness

The client needs to have an **expectation** that they will be hypnotized, and they have to know what will happen. If you just told someone who has never been hypnotized, "Go into hypnosis NOW!" Well... how do they know what that's supposed to mean? They have never been hypnotized before; they don't know what to do. The RIF creates a positive expectation in the client.

The client also needs **motivation** to be hypnotized, especially if there will be a change. We create positive motivation by simply outlining the benefits of being hypnotized.

Once the client has a motivation to go into hypnosis, they will look forward to the experience, thus allowing hypnosis to occur much easier.

Next, the client needs to **believe** that they can do this. Often, people will say, "I don't know if I can be hypnotized." Creating a firm belief in the client's mind that hypnosis will surely happen for them is crucial—and it is also taken care of in the RIF.

Using the RIF keeps the client informed at all times. By ensuring that they know what is going to happen, you convince them that they are going to enjoy the rapid hypnotic induction process and that it will work perfectly for them. This creates **willingness** on their part. The client must be willing to follow your instructions and must be willing to be hypnotized.

CHAPTER 4

Rapid Or Instant?

What is a rapid induction? What is an instant induction? Most hypnotists would agree to define an **instant induction** is—exactly that—one that happens (or should happen) in three seconds or less. A **rapid induction** is still fast but can typically takes up to three minutes. Despite agreement on the general term, there is a debate in the hypnosis community: are rapid and instant inductions really "instantaneous"? This question arises because the actual induction does not start when the hypnotist says, "sleep!" The induction starts with the pre-talk. You may be accustomed to pre-talks that last 15 minutes, but you can still do a pre-talk and all the steps of my Rapid Induction Formula in three minutes or less.

Perhaps, on television or in YouTube videos, you have seen a hypnotist walk up to a stranger on the street, shake their hand and shout, "SLEEP!" The next thing you see is that the person crumbles to the ground. I can't tell you how many emails and messages I get from people asking me to teach them how to do this. Here's the truth: There has to be some setup to that. The chances of just walking up to a random person on the street, slamming them instantly into a trance, so they crumble to the ground—is slim to none.

So... do instant inductions *really* exist, given that the induction *actually* starts as soon as the hypnotist starts talking? What is your perspective?

NOTE: In my stage shows, it appears to the audience as if I am hypnotizing a whole group of 20 participants in about 30 seconds. In reality, the entire process takes about 15 minutes, including the pre-talk and pre-framing, which sets the expectation of what will happen to get to the point of rapidly hypnotizing the people who volunteer for the show. But it still looks pretty fancy. If you want to see a live demonstration of my Rapid Induction Formula onstage, go to:
www.RapidInductionFormula.com/Resources

CHAPTER 5

The RAPID Benefit

I am often asked why I prefer rapid inductions; sometimes, I am even criticized for using them. Whether you use them or not is up to you, but you should have them in your toolbox and know how and why they work. So, why should *you* use rapid inductions?

When I was taught stage hypnosis, I learned, essentially, how to read a script and do a progressive relaxation induction. I did several shows using that induction. I found people would get bored, and I didn't really understand why the progressive relaxation induction worked. When did it start? When did it end? After a year or two of using this long, drawn-out induction, I saw a hypnotist at a county fair do a group hand-lock[1], and then instantly hypnotize the group of volunteers on stage. As my jaw dropped, the audience gasped so loud that they sucked all of the air out of the fairgrounds.

After seeing that hypnotist instantly hypnotize his volunteers, I was addicted to rapid inductions. I learned everything that I could about them.

Here are some of my reasons to use rapid inductions:

First and foremost, they are impressive. These inductions instantly position you as an authority in hypnosis. After each stage show I do, I ask the client why they booked me over other hypnotists. Most of them say two things... "We book you because you're fast and funny."

---

[1] The hand-lock is a concentration exercise that you will learn later in this book.

Dan Candell's Rapid Induction Formula

Onstage, rapid inductions allow you to get into the show faster; rapid inductions look more impressive and are more dramatic—it's a show, after all, let's give people what they came for! They also help overcome the misconceptions of the audience that hypnosis is a long, drawn-out process. (It can be, but it doesn't have to be.)

Another reason to do rapid inductions is that you can do them anywhere, anytime. Imagine giving a lecture about hypnosis, and someone raises their hand and asks, "can you hypnotize me now?" If you bring them up and do a progressive relaxation induction, it would take too long, it would bore the audience to tears, and it would appear to the audience that you are just relaxing the volunteer.

Now, imagine that same scenario. But instead, you bring the volunteers up in front of the group, and you hypnotize them from sitting up to slumped over in about 20 seconds and start doing an arm catalepsy or eyelid catalepsy. **That** looks pretty impressive, doesn't it? It also builds your reputation much faster.

Moving away from stage shows and demonstrations: why should you use rapid inductions, or at least know them, for private clients? Have you ever had a client talk so much in the early parts of the session that you barely have any time left to hypnotize them? Or, what if a client came in late and you still wanted to do a hypnosis session? What if you planned a longer change process, and you needed the client to go into hypnosis quickly so that you have more time for that change process? These are all good times to pull out the good ole rapid induction formula.

NOTE: The Rapid Induction Formula can be used on stage, as a street hypnosis demonstration, in groups, in noisy settings, and in a clinical setting with private hypnosis clients.

CHAPTER 6

Avoid The TRAP

Why Most Hypnotists Don't Use Rapid Inductions

After speaking at a hypnosis conference, I polled people about why most hypnotists fall into the trap and don't use rapid inductions. Here were the responses:

1) The hypnotist lacks confidence in *their* ability to hypnotize someone quickly.

2) The hypnotist is afraid that the induction will fail; thus, it will look like they failed.

3) Rapid inductions are too dramatic and showy and don't belong in a clinical setting.

4) The inductions look too violent.

Let's face it; most hypnotists are first taught the same way I was… how to read a script. But, all too often, they don't know how or why the script works. There is no real script for rapid inductions. Instead, they are process-driven. It follows, then, that many hypnotists don't do rapid inductions simply because they don't think they can do them, especially without a script. Believe me, though, it takes more guts to go in front of a group of 600 people and do a boring 20-minute progressive relaxation induction than it does to do a rapid induction.

This lack of confidence usually leads to the concern or fear that the induction will fail, and it will look bad for the hypnotist.
This could possibly even cause the client to doubt that they can be hypnotized. Let's workshop this. What happens if you do **any** induction, and the client says, "I don't think I was hypnotized?" This objection is always traced back to the pre-talk that we do with

Dan Candell's Rapid Induction Formula

clients and how we set the frame. My goal with this Rapid Induction Formula is to teach you how to avoid these concerns and fears so that you feel confident and comfortable doing rapid inductions.

Rapid inductions aren't just for stage shows. I have also heard a different variation of this objection. I have heard several hypnotists say, "I want my clients to enjoy the process of going into hypnosis, so I take 20-30 minutes to hypnotize them to make sure they enjoy it." I call that whole thing BS. In my clinic, after hypnotizing thousands of clients, people enjoy hypnosis just as much, if not, more with an induction that takes just three minutes as they would enjoy a 30-minute induction. If you don't believe me, test it out.

A huge misconception about rapid inductions is that they have to be dramatic or forceful. People sometimes think that you have to yank someone's arm or jerk their body to get them into hypnosis.

A fellow hypnotist had the belief that when doing an arm pull induction, the harder you yank their arm, the deeper into hypnosis they will go. He was doing a hypnosis show for a party and had a woman onstage. She wasn't going into hypnosis, so he kept yanking her arm harder and harder, and she kept saying, "OUCH! YOU'RE GOING TO RIP MY ARM OUT OF THE SOCKET!"

I am going to give you a bit of wisdom here... DON'T DO THAT!

In this book, you will learn rapid inductions that are permissive, and you will learn rapid inductions that are authoritative. Both work equally as well. And no, you don't have to scream "SLEEP" at someone and yank them to the ground...

Before we get to the formula, let's cover some preludes to the induction: concentration exercises!

NOTE: There are two ways to induce hypnosis. One is by *overloading* the nervous system, and the other is by *relaxing or fatiguing* the nervous system.

CHAPTER 7

Hypnotic Experiences & Exercises

Many hypnotists used to call these *suggestibility tests*; however, I highly recommend that you use the terminology *concentration exercise* or *hypnotic experience*. The term "suggestibility test" has the negative implication that a person must be gullible to be hypnotized, which as we know, is not true.

The purpose of doing concentration exercises is to find out which people are going to react the best and be most responsive to hypnosis. You are looking for people who are following your instructions and who are compliant.

Even if you are doing a group demo, this will give your attendees a hypnotic experience as these exercises are hypnotic in nature.

These exercises also serve the purpose to warm up the group or client, to give them a hypnotic experience, to build rapport and compliance, and to knock down resistance. Their responses will also to give you an idea of what kind of hypnotic subject they will be. If they comply with the tests and perform well, then they will usually be easy to hypnotize and prime candidates for the Rapid Induction Formula.

Magnetic Fingers

This one is a very common exercise. There is some debate in the hypnosis community whether this exercise should be considered "hypnosis" because it is an automatic physical reaction. My opinion is that it is a good tool to measure compliance because a person can resist this and keep it from happening. You are looking for those people who comply, not those who resist.

It can be spoken like this:

"Everyone clasp your hands tight together and make sure your palms are touching. Now

extend your two index fingers like this..." (Show them what to do.)

"Good, now in a moment I am going to count forward from 1 to 3; on my count of three, I want you to do three things. The first thing you're going to do is look at your fingers, then you're going to separate your two index fingers, and then you are going to listen to my voice. And you are going to see something amazing happen."

"One... Two... Three. "

"Now, look at your fingers; separate your index fingers. They are going to touch. Imagine that space between them is getting smaller and smaller until they touch. Like magnets or rubber bands are attached to your fingers. It may happen slowly; it may happen fast."

Continue in this way until you start seeing people's fingers touching. You can even suggest to them that they will touch faster the second time. You can use this exercise to tell them that when they let it happen, and they think about what they want to happen, it will happen.

And hypnosis works in much the same way.

Hand Lock Exercise

This is a favorite exercise among stage hypnotists because when used in the right place, and delivered in the right way, it can be very powerful. Unlike many exercises, tests, or convincers, this one is actually a challenge. Therefore, it works best when done in an authoritative way. It can also be used as the induction itself, as you will see later in this book.

Start off by having people clasp their hands tight together, interlacing their fingers. Mirror them to show them what they should be doing. You then suggest that their hands are squeezing tighter and tighter together. You suggest to them that as you count forward from 1 to 5, their hands will lock together, and no matter how hard they try, they will not be able to take their hands apart.

The wording should go something like this:

"Everybody, clasp your hands together, interlocking your fingers."

"Focus on the point where your thumbs cross."

"In a moment, I'll count forward from 1 to 5. On my count of five, your hands will be locked together, and you will not be able to open

Dan Candell's Rapid Induction Formula

them no matter how hard you try. They will lock tighter and tighter with each and every number that I count."

"One, squeeze your hands tighter and tighter, locking them, mashing them, melting them together. Your hands are cramping and clamping together as if they were in a vice."

"Two, as you feel the blood pulsing through your fingers, and see the whiteness of your knuckles, your hands only squeeze, lock, mash, melt, and go tighter and tighter together."

"Three, think to yourself, my hands are locked, my hands are locked, my hands are locked. Many of you have already locked your hands together. But don't try to take them apart yet. Let them keep squeezing tighter and tighter together as if they were glued, bolted, or magnetized together."

"Four, now it becomes a reality, anything you have to do to imagine your hands will not come apart happens right now. Your hands are locked; they are locked tightly and firmly together."

"Five, now the harder you try, the tighter they will get. Your hands are locked, locked, locked tight together."

"Now stop trying to take them apart but leave them locked until I release you."

At this point, you release their hands simply by counting forward from 1 to 3 and suggesting their hands relax and melt apart.

Special Keys To Note About This Exercise

- Notice the imagery that is in the process. Use words such as "stuck, glued, clamped, magnetized." By suggesting this, you are evoking many thoughts that suggest their hands will stay together.

- Throughout the exercise, using words such as "try to take your hands apart," suggests a failure in their mind.

- At the end of the exercise, when the subject(s) attempt to take their hands apart, I only let them try for a couple of seconds unless I have more than enough volunteers on stage (if I am doing a stage show).

- If you are doing a stage show or a group demonstration and you have an overabundance of volunteers, you may want to weed more people out to narrow down your group to a more manageable size.

Arms Rising And Falling

This exercise is more permissive, and it is also a good visual indicator of how receptive each potential subject will be.

If you have people perform this exercise while they are standing, instruct them to stand with their feet shoulders' width apart, and to maintain balance to be sure that they do not fall. Depending on how long this exercise takes to complete, you may see many people swaying.

Have everyone extend their left arm out in front of them with their palm facing the ceiling. Have them extend their right arm out in front of them with their palm facing the ground. Have them close their eyes. I find this exercise works better if you have people tilt their head slightly back towards the ceiling, which throws off their equilibrium, making this even more effective.

You can continue like this:

"Bring your attention over to your left hand."

"Imagine in your left hand; I just placed a very heavy bowling ball. This bowling ball is pulling your left arm down towards the ground. It gets heavier and heavier and heavier." (Use inflection in your voice to suggest heaviness.)

"As your arm gets heavier and heavier, it lowers down towards the ground." (At this point, you should start seeing their left arm slowly moving down.)

"Now, bring your imagination and concentration over to your right hand."

"Imagine I tied 5,000 helium balloons to your right arm, and it begins to rise. It's getting lighter and higher, higher lighter." (Use inflection in your voice to suggest "lightness." As you talk, your voice should get higher and lighter.)

"The higher your right arm gets, the lower your left arm gets." (You should see their right arm rising and their left arm continuing to get lower.)

Be sure that you use inflection as you're talking to reinforce the suggested heaviness and lightness.

During this exercise, look for movements that are slow and sluggish. When you start talking about the bowling ball, if a person's left arm immediately drops by their side and they start giggling, it usually means they are forcing it to happen, and they will not be good hypnotic subjects. The same thing is true for the right hand. If when you suggest the balloons in the right hand, and their right arm shoots straight up instantly, then they are usually trying to force it.

Posture Sway

This exercise can be very intimidating for hypnotists who are of smaller stature.

Caution should be taken when performing this exercise with women. You want to make sure that nobody feels violated. I have seen some male hypnotists have a female subject fall forward into their arms and then make a tasteless joke. This unprofessionalism undermines your authority and alienates participants.

You want to avoid performing this exercise with people who are wearing flip-flops, heels, or high boots, so use this with people who are wearing flat-footed shoes such as sneakers or running shoes.

Have the person stand in front of you, with their feet together and their arms resting loose and limp by their sides. As with many concentration exercises, having the subject look up towards the ceiling and close their eyes will throw off their equilibrium, and we can use that to our advantage.

Instruct them to look up and close their eyes. The change in equilibrium may cause them to start to sway back and forth.

Tell them that as you count backward from 3 to 1, they will start to fall backward.

Tell them not to catch themselves.

Make sure that you are positioned behind them, and that you have your dominant leg anchoring you. Position your legs far apart, to make sure that you can catch them.

Then, suggest they start falling backward.

You should only let them fall about 6 inches. This will feel like a greater distance to them.

The response you are looking for is to have them fall back naturally without catching themselves and without hesitation. If they catch themselves, it means that they are afraid or don't trust that you will catch them.

Arm Catalepsy As A Concentration Exercise

This exercise is what I use 95 percent of the time to lead into the Rapid Induction Formula. This exercise requires more of an authoritative approach. Have the participants extend their left arm out in front of them and focus on a spot on their hand.

"On my count of 3, put your left arm out in front of you and focus on one spot on your left hand... 1, 2, 3!"

"Allow all of your focus and concentration to zone in on that hand."

"Now, the next time I count to three, make a tight fist with your left hand."

"As you do, your left arm will become stiff and rigid. So stiff and so rigid that you won't be able to bend it no matter how hard you try!"

"1, 2, 3! Make that tight fist and make your arm stiff and rigid."

"Make it so stiff and rigid that if I tried to bend it, it stays stiff and rigid and cannot

bend!" (At this point, test the participants by grasping their wrist and testing the rigidity of their arm. As you test their arm, reassure them by saying things like, "good, this is not a test of strength, but a test of concentration, imagination and focus!)

"Now, make that arm so stiff and so rigid that YOU cannot bend it even if YOU tried! Go ahead and test it for yourself, that arm is STIFF AND RIGID!"

When conducting this exercise, start with the easiest command first, which is having them make their arm so stiff that YOU cannot bend it, and then pace them into making it now so THEY can't bend it.

CHAPTER 8

The Nuts And Bolts

Dan Candell's Signature Rapid Induction Formula

While developing this formula, I tested various inductions and variations over the years. I found that most of the rapid inductions use very similar methods. I'm going to outline several different instant inductions that you can use after a concentration exercise, but first, I will explain the overall approach and the four common elements of my signature Rapid Induction Formula.

Because the formula is a **formula**, it is done in basically the same way, regardless of the specific induction and regardless of which concentration exercise is used. The formula goes a little something like this:

Pre-frame + Concentration Exercise + Sleep Talk + Trigger = Deep Hypnosis

Pre-frame: This is where you demonstrate what hypnosis is going to be, and you build confidence in the client that:

1) You can do hypnosis quickly, and

2) They can go into hypnosis quickly.

Concentration Exercise: This is a simple exercise[2] such as the hand-lock, magnetic fingers, eye catalepsy, or arms rising and falling. Some of these have been included in this book, but the formula works with your choice of exercise. You use the exercise as an interlude into the induction.

NOTE: It's important to explain every step of the way – "immediately following this exercise, I am going to place you deep into hypnosis."

---

[2] See the previous section for my thoughts about calling these "exercises" not "tests". Many hypnotists and web sites will still use the term "suggestibility test".

Sleep Talk: This is where you explain exactly what is going to happen in order for them to go deep into hypnosis. *"Now, when I touch you on the shoulder or hand and say the word 'SLEEP', your body will just melt, relax and collapse, and you'll instantly relax right into a deep instant hypnosis relaxation."*

Trigger: Finally, you now touch them on the shoulder or the forehead, or do a gentle arm tug, and say "SLEEP." The trigger should match what you described in the sleep talk.

Looking Deeper Into The Pre-frame

The first element is the pre-frame. You can look at the pre-frame as a simplified pre-talk, or you can see it as "setting the stage" for all that follows. In the pre-frame, you tell them exactly what *you* are going to do, and exactly what *they* are going to do. You also set the foundation that **you are the hypnotist** and that **you do rapid hypnosis**.

You must get the client in agreement that they can and will be hypnotized quickly.

A typical pre-frame might sound a little like this:

"You know I am a hypnotist." – Establish authority and set your identity as the hypnotist

"I do it a little differently, though; I do what's called rapid hypnosis." – Set the expectation that you are going to do rapid hypnosis.

"I am going to hypnotize you using a very quick and effective method." - Are you onboard? – Get them to agree.

"All you have to do is follow my very simple instructions." – Building compliance.

"I will have you do a few simple things, and when you follow my instructions, your eyes will close, and you'll let your body slump down and relax." – Pre-framing their responses.

"Then, your subconscious mind opens up to accept my positive messages to you." – Leading and pacing them for what is going to happen once they are hypnotized.

"You literally instantly relax—like your entire body just exhaled, and a wave of heaviness goes through your body."
– Establishing what their experience will be like

Sound good? – Getting them into a more agreeable state

The whole pre-frame takes under a minute. It can be done in 30 to 60 seconds. It should be delivered in a quick and fluid manner. When I am telling them how they are going to respond and what hypnosis will be like, I also mirror with my body how they will respond. When I tell them, "you will slump down and relax," I make my body slump so they can actually see how they should respond. It is also wise that you make sure the client or participant does not have any neck, shoulder, or back injuries. If they do, you want to avoid any sudden jerking movements to their arm, heard, or neck.

Once you get the client or group in agreement, you can move into a concentration exercise, discussed next.

Sometimes though, you will need to add a little more to the pre-frame in order to clear up some myths and misconceptions of hypnosis. If you sense any resistance, it means you need to add a little more of an explanation.

Here are some common myths and misconceptions that you may need to clear up before continuing on with the process.

- Fear of not being emerged or getting stuck in hypnosis

- Hypnosis is mind control

- You will lose control when you're hypnotized

- You will divulge secrets while you're hypnotized

- Hypnosis is sleep or being unconscious

- You have to be gullible or weak-willed to be hypnotized

There are a few ways you can handle these myths and misconceptions. You can just address these concerns by reframing them and educating your client or audience, or you can accomplish the same thing in a more fun and entertaining way.

I find it much more beneficial to clear up these myths and misconceptions while I am telling a story. You can tell a story about how someone asked a ridiculous question about what happens if we get stuck in hypnosis, and then laugh about it. People will remember a story much better than they will remember straight facts. Use your own personal experience to make the pre-frame more fun and entertaining.

Looking Deeper Into The Concentration Exercise

All of these inductions in the rapid induction formula continue with a concentration exercise.

After a concentration exercise, the group or clients are in a more receptive and more compliant state, so they will continue to follow your instructions. This is where you will pace them and give them further instructions for going into hypnosis.

NOTE: As I mentioned earlier, the old term "suggestibility test" has negative connotations, so I never call it a test to my clients because I don't want them to know or think I am testing them. I just explain it as, "we are going to do a little mental exercise that will help me hypnotize you very quickly."

There are several concentration exercises that you can do with either a group or an individual. Nowadays, I usually start off with arm catalepsy if I am working with a group onstage. In the office, I take a slightly gentler approach, and I do an eye lock.[3]

Here are some exercises you can do, which will lead into the induction:

1) **Arm catalepsy** – having the client(s) believe that their arm is still and rigid and they can't bend it

2) **Eye lock** – having the client(s) think their eyelids are locked or glued closed

3) **Hand lock** – having the client(s) think that their hands are locked together.

4) **Arms rising and falling** – having the client(s) think one arm is very light and starts to lift, and the other arm is very heavy and starts to pull down.

5) **Hand to face** – having the client(s) think there is a magnet on their palm and another on their face resulting in their outstretched hand moving in towards their face.

---

[3] The more clinical term for eye-lock is "eye catalepsy." You can see a demonstration for this by going to www.RapidInductionFormula.com/Resources

Dan Candell's Rapid Induction Formula

6) **Finger magnets** – having the client(s) think there are magnets on their two outstretched fingers, and they move in together until they touch.

There are many other concentration exercises from which you can choose.

The primary purpose of the concentration exercise is to start creating hypnotic experiences for the client and to build compliance within the client. This leads them into a more receptive hypnotic state.

NOTE: Keep in mind that this is all a process that should flow together. It can be done in either an authoritative or a permissive manner. You should adapt all of this to fit your style and personality.

Looking Deeper Into The Sleep Talk

At the end of the successful completion of a concentration test, you present what I call the "sleep talk." This is a method that I use for a group:

"It is now time to go into that deep receptive state and be deeply instantly hypnotized."

"In a moment I'm going to come around to each one of you and touch you on the hand, the head, or the shoulder and say the word, 'sleep!'"

"The moment I touch you and say 'sleep!' your eyes will close, your entire body will go loose and limp like a ragdoll, and your head will drop forward or on to the person next to you, and you'll be deeply instantly hypnotized."

"The moment I touch you, your eyes will close, and your entire body will instantly relax and collapse like a ragdoll."

"You will be deeply instantly hypnotized, and no matter how deeply relaxed you go, you will always stay in your chair and always hear the sound of my voice."

You may notice the use of "power words" like "and" rather than "but", and that some of the instructions are repeated. As with all hypnotic language, make your word choice deliberate.

If I am doing this with only one person, I will usually alter the sleep talk instructions a little to suit the individual. It may sound like this:

"Now that you have followed my instructions, and you are doing great, in a moment I will just push your hand(s) down and say the word "sleep!" Instantly, just let your eyes close and let your body just sink down into a really heavy and deep state of relaxation."

Looking Deeper Into The Trigger

At this point, I go around and give a slight tug on their hand or arm and say the word "sleep!" This is the hypnosis trigger.

You should be looking for them to relax instantly, and their bodies should become very heavy, loose, and limp with their muscles sagged down. Many times, you'll often see signs of REM (rapid eye movement) with their eyes fluttering, and often their neck area may turn a beet red color, these are signs of a deep hypnotic state.

Putting It Into Practice

In this section, you will see a variety of inductions that use the Rapid Induction Formula. These can be applied to groups and to individuals. They can also be adapted to suit your style. If you prefer a more permissive method, you can deliver them in a gentler way. If you prefer a more authoritative method, you can be more commanding and direct.

NOTE: For simplicity, I refer to "participants" rather than volunteer, subject, client, or victim (of course I am joking!) in these examples. This term can include stage volunteers, hypnotherapy clients, or your Great Aunt Mary, who you are hypnotizing at the family reunion. Some inductions are more suited to groups; others may be more individual. The formula works the same way each time.

Dan Candell's Rapid Induction Formula

The Rigid Arm Induction

This induction is based on a subconscious overload principle that does not allow the participants to analyze everything that is happening. This induction should be done with the participants seated. It is done in a more authoritative style. There is a cadence to it where it should be done rapidly.

Begin with the **pre-frame** (1), as described earlier.

Have the participants each extend their left arm in front of them and instruct them to focus at one spot on their left hand. Suggest to them that you will count to three, and on your count of three, they will make a tight fist with their left hand, and as they do, their left arm will go stiff and rigid like a steel bar of iron. This is the **concentration exercise** (2).

See how it comes together:

"In a moment, I'm going to count forward from 1 to 3."

"And when I do, put your left arm out in front of you as far as it will go."

"One, two, three. Great!"

"Now focus on one spot on your left hand. It could be a finger, fingernail, freckle, or knuckle. But stare at one spot on your hand and do not look away from that spot."

"Now, I'll count to three one more time, and when I do, make a tight fist with your left hand."

"The moment you make that tight fist, let your left arm go stiff and rigid like a steel bar of iron. No matter how hard you try to bend it, it will not bend."

"One. Two. Three: stiff and rigid!"

At this point, I go around and test their arms just by giving them a slight push in saying, "stiff and rigid" as I touch their arm. You also want to reassure them by using words such as, "good, that's right, exactly, just like that." In a stage setting, you can also use this point to dismiss anyone that you do not think is following your suggestions.

Proceed and give the **sleep talk** (3) with the hypnotic instructions.

Then, simply, go to each participant and just touch their hand that is extended, as you say the **trigger** (4), the word *sleep*.

Dan Candell's Rapid Induction Formula

Because you have given the proper instructions, their eyes now close, their heads drop down on the person next to them, and their bodies instantly relax.

The participants have now entered deep hypnosis.

CHAPTER 9

The Glue That Brings It Together

The Hand Lock Induction

This induction should be done with participants seated.

1. You should begin with the **pre-frame** (1).

2. Follow with the hand lock **concentration exercise** (2).

3. Then include the **sleep talk** (3) immediately following the hand lock exercise.

Dan Candell's Rapid Induction Formula

You go around to each participant who has their hands locked, and you issue the **trigger** (4) by pushing their hands down into their lap as you say the word "sleep!"

This process, using this formula, causes a deep hypnotic response.

Posture Sway/Standing Induction

This induction should be done with a participant who is standing. This is usually done with male participants and should not be done with people who are predisposed to injury. This induction should be done in a forceful and authoritative manner where you are taking command.

In many stage shows, I often start with this induction, as I have a few people standing on stage in front of the people seated in chairs.

NOTE: Precautions should be taken when performing this induction. I do not recommend performing this type of induction unless you've had a lot of practice and experience and are confident that everyone involved will remain very safe and secure.

Dan Candell's Rapid Induction Formula

Begin with the **pre-frame** (1), which in a stage show setting may be done with the entire audience.

To start the **concentration exercise** (2), I will have each person standing put their feet together, their arms loosely and limply by their sides, and I will have them tilt their head back, focusing on one spot on the ceiling.

Speaking directly to the participant (off-mic in a show), instruct them to *"Stand with your feet together, and your hands loosely and limply by your sides."*

At this point, you can pick up their arms and make sure when you drop them; they just drop right back by their sides with no resistance.

Continue: *"Tilt your head back towards the ceiling and fix your eyes on one spot on the ceiling, and do not look away from that spot."*

At this point, I continue on with the next couple of people that I have standing so that the first person can be left alone for 30 to 60 seconds focusing on the spot.

I then return back to that person that I started with and give them an abbreviated version of the **sleep talk** (3). This sounds something like this:

"In a moment, I'm going to say the word sleep, and when I do, you'll let your entire body fall straight back into my arms, and I will catch you."

"As soon as I say the word sleep, your eyes will close, and your entire body will fall straight back into my arms, and you will be deeply instantly hypnotized."

"When I lower you to the ground, your body will go loose and limp."

Then, simply saying the word "sleep" acts as the **trigger** (4).

If you are doing this induction, make sure you are very prepared because sometimes people will not fall straight backward—instead, their entire body can just collapse downward, and you have to be prepared to catch them.

NOTE: You can see a demonstration of this induction performed onstage by visiting the resource page for this book:
www.RapidInductionFormula.com/resources

Monkey See Monkey Do Induction

This is an induction that I developed just recently.

After I do the posture sway induction (usually for dramatic effect), I will go up to the people who are seated. Keep in mind that the **pre-frame** (1) has been given to the whole group, and they may have been involved in an earlier **concentration exercise** (2) in the audience. Even if not, they have been close to and paying rapt attention to the extremely recent posture sway induction directly in front of them.

This lets me jump right into the **sleep talk** (3), and say:

"Now, when I tap you on the head and say 'sleep', the same thing that happened to those people will happen to you, except you will stay in your chair..."

And then, I can immediately use the **trigger** (4) and say "sleep" as I tap them on the head.

Remember, a big part of hypnosis is expectancy, and when you hypnotize someone in front of several others who are waiting to be hypnotized, they now know what to expect. However, this can sometimes backfire if the person you are using as an example does not get hypnotized rapidly (or at all!) In such a case, don't use this Monkey See, Monkey Do technique.

The Progressive Eye Lock Induction

This induction can be stretched out to take 3 to 5 minutes. If you would like a slightly longer and less dramatic induction, this is the one I recommend that you do.

Begin, as always, with a **pre-frame** (1).

The **concentration exercise** (2) starts off with participants seated.

Dan Candell's Rapid Induction Formula

Have them look up at the ceiling and focus on one spot. You can then have them close their eyes on a downward count for a more dramatic and relaxing effect.

Once their eyes are closed, you can perform an eye catalepsy by doing another downward count.

Once they achieve relaxation and catalepsy in their eyelids, and they test that feeling (similar to an abbreviated Elman induction), you can do a brief physical relaxation or body scan.

Once the body scan is complete, and they appear to be relaxing, you can give the **sleep talk** and do a slight tug of the arm to **trigger** the hypnosis. (See below)

It can be performed like this:

"Everybody sit back in your chairs with your feet on the floor. Now, look up towards the ceiling and focus on one spot on the ceiling."

"As you look at that spot, let your eyes get very heavy so that they want to close. But do not close them until I count backward from 5 to 1. When I reach the number one, or before, close your eyes down."

"Five, letting your eyes get so very heavy they want to close."

"Four, letting your eyes relax more and more with every number."

"Three, letting your eyes feel so heavy, they may begin to blink and water."

"Two, wanting to close those eyes."

"And one, close your eyes shutting out all the light."

Now you can continue on with an eye-lock:

"Now that your eyes are closed, relax them so much, so they have no desire to open."

"Imagine that I placed glue under your closed eyelids."

"Let them feel like lead weights are pressing down on your eyelids."

"As I count backward from 5 to 1, your eyelids will feel so heavy that they won't be able to open."

"Five, letting those eyes feel so heavy like they're glued shut."

Dan Candell's Rapid Induction Formula

"Four, letting those eyelids get so heavy like there are lead weights attached to them."

"Three, so heavy they don't want to open, it feels like they are locked shut."

"Two, they are so tightly closed they will not open."

"One, eyes are so tightly shut they will not open even if you tried. Stop trying and keep your eyes closed, now."

Now you can continue with a very brief physical relaxation.

"Take that same feeling of relaxation that's in your eyelids and let it go down through your body like a wave."

"As I count backward from 5 to 1 one more time, let your head get so very heavy that it just wants to drop forward. As I count backward, let your head get so heavy it begins to roll forward like you are trying to touch your chin to your chest."

"By the time I reach the number one or before, just let your head drop down like it weighs 1000 pounds."

"Five, letting your head get so very heavy, it just begins to roll forward now."

"Four, your head is so very heavy and so very tired that you can't keep it up anymore."

"Three, your head is rolling forward now as all of the muscles in your neck also relax."

"Two, letting your head just roll forward now."

"On my final count, let your head just drop forward, and the moment it does let your entire body instantly relax."

"ONE! Deep relaxation."

Now, this is where you can insert the **sleep talk** (3), and again proceed with a slight gentle arm tug that will **trigger** (4) a deeper state of hypnosis.

Dan Candell's Rapid Induction Formula

CHAPTER 10

Get Them Deeper

One of the biggest mistakes that people make when doing rapid inductions is after the trigger, they don't follow up immediately with a deepener. Sometimes, the hypnotist will be so surprised that the induction worked that they just stop talking! Make sure to always follow up with a deepener immediately following the induction.

In this section, you will learn several quick and easy deepeners that will do the job.

Fractionation As A Deepener

Fractionation in hypnosis is when you have the hypnotized individual or group come out of hypnosis and then go back into hypnosis. Each time they come out of hypnosis, they go even deeper, each time that they return to the hypnotic trance state.

When you think about it, an entire hypnosis stage show is essentially based on fractionation. You have them emerge and do a skit and then relax back down after the skit. Each time this happens, they are going deeper into hypnosis. So, in theory, the routines can get more challenging and complex as the show goes on.

That's why you usually start with simpler routines in the beginning of the show and move on to routines that require a deeper level of hypnosis as the show progresses. Fractionation *can be* a very entertaining and effective way to deepen the hypnotic state.

The following technique came from the modified Elman induction. For this deepener, you should have a microphone stand, or water bottle, or something else placed in the center of the stage and positioned in front of the participants so they can all focus on it. In a one-on-one setting, any object that can be placed in the participant's field of view will work. This technique goes something like this:

"In a moment, I'm going to count to three."

"Only on my count of three, you will all sit up and open your eyes, and you will look at the microphone stand that is on the stage in front of you."

"Then, when you hear me say the words SLEEP NOW, your eyes will instantly close, and you will relax and collapse back into hypnosis."

"Every time we do this, you'll relax 100 times more."

"One, two, three. Eyes open and look at the mic stand."

"Good, SLEEP NOW!"

Arm Levitation Deepener

You can use this deepener at the beginning of a stage show, or individual session, immediately following the induction, or you can also use it later to deepen hypnosis, perhaps after an intermission in a show, or if you see a participant beginning to rouse themselves.

You suggest to the participants that both of their arms feel very light and will begin to rise into the air. The higher their arms get, the more relaxed they become.
For an added comedic effect in a show, you can suggest that their arms feel so light that they will pull them right out of the chair. When they are standing, you can suggest that their arms will be stuck in that elevated position, and they will not be able to move their arms. Have them open their eyes and ask them what is happening, the responses that you get will be outstanding.

Explain that the only time they can move their arms is when you snap your fingers, (or snap your fingers next to their ears, and do this to each individual person).

Dan Candell's Rapid Induction Formula

NOTE: If you have the participants do the arms rising and falling exercise as a concentration test earlier, then this exercise can be repetitive, so I do not use both in the same show or session.

The Everything Deepener

This deepener is a good one to use when you need a quick deepener that compounds as time goes on throughout the entire show or session.

It sounds like this:

"From this point onward in the show, anything you do, see, hear or feel will only help you go deeper and deeper into the hypnotic state."

NOTE: Quite often in a stage show, I will layer deepeners for added effect. For example, I may start off with an intermittent counting deepener,[4] such as the "Counting" or "Staircase" deepeners that, then go on to a breath deepener,[5] and then go on to this everything deepener.

---

[4] Intermittent counting is when the hypnotist counts and reinforces a suggestion, or even gives a new suggestion, between each number. Both the "Counting" example and the "Staircase" example in this section use intermittent counting.

[5] A "breath deepener" is something simple like: *"Every breath you exhale takes you deeper."*

Counting

You can do a very simple downward count from ten to one, or five to one to deepen the hypnotic state.

You suggest to the participants that every number you count helps them relax more and more. It can sound something like this:

"As I count from 5 to 1, you will double your relaxation with every number."

"5... Deeper down. Every breath you exhale helps you go deeper."

"4... More relaxed now, doubling your relaxation."
"3... Every sound you hear sending you even deeper down no"

*"2... All the way down now like a wave of relaxation went from the top of your head to the tips of your toes ....
now on ..."*

"1! Sleep deeper now!"

Dan Candell's Rapid Induction Formula

The Staircase Deepener

This is one of the most traditional and popular deeners that hypnotists use. It starts by having the participants thinking that they are standing on the top of a staircase and having them walk down each step in their mind. Every step that they take causes them to go deeper into the hypnotic state.

It can be presented like this:

"Now that you're responding wonderfully to my previous instructions, I am going to help you go deeper into this state of hypnotic receptivity."

"You have relaxed your body, and now it is time to relax your mind by giving your mind something to do."

"Imagine, picture, visualize, or even just thinking about being on the top of a beautiful staircase. This particular set of stairs has ten steps."

"As I count down from ten to one, take another step down with every number."

"Each step is a number, and each number is a step."

"Each step you take and every number that I count will help you go even deeper into this wonderful hypnotic receptive state."

"By the time I get to the number one, you will be open and receptive to my suggestions and instructions..."

At this point, you can count down from ten to one slowly, or you can use intermittent counting, like this:

"10... take that first step down, and just allow yourself to go even deeper

9... take that next step down and let your mind drift and dream and flow

8... allowing your mind to open even more

7... enjoying every moment of this process

6... feeling better with every gentle breath you exhale

5... every number I count, every word I say, helping you go even deeper now
4... entering into that perfect state of receptive relaxation

3... all the way down

Dan Candell's Rapid Induction Formula

2... take one more deep breath now... and...

1... all the way down, just sinks deeper down now, allowing your mind to open and it also drifts and dreams and wonders."

Note: You may notice that I say, "Imagine, picture, visualize, bring your mind to, or at least just think about..." when I want a client to have something in mind because not everyone is visual. "Think about or bring your mind to," helps those people who are not always able to imagine or picture things.

CHAPTER 11

Wakey, Wakey!

There are many thoughts of the wording used when you bring someone out of hypnosis.

Since a person isn't asleep while they are hypnotized, is it appropriate to say, "wake up"? I have found, especially specifically with individual clients, that if I say, "wake up," people question if they have been hypnotized—because they were not asleep. Using the words "wake up" or "awake" can pre-suppose that they were sleeping.

Instead, we say "emerge from" or "come out of" hypnosis.

If you are bringing participants in a stage show or demonstration out of hypnosis, it is important to remove all of the suggestions

Dan Candell's Rapid Induction Formula

you gave them. Say something like, "when you come out of hypnosis, everything I told you is erased, and you will be back to normal. You will remember as much or as little as you need or want to."

If you are emerging a client from a private session, you want to make sure you reinforce everything you told them by saying something like, "Upon emerging, everything I told you will become your reality and will be deeply reinforced."

After you give them the necessary suggestions, you can emerge them by using a simple counting out.

"One, take a nice deep breath and feel the energy surging through your body now."

"Two, sitting up and feeling yourself becoming clearer and more alert."

"Three, feeling absolutely fantastic about everything. Sitting up and stretching out as if you just woke up from a nice long nap."

"Four, taking in another nice deep breath of fresh air and letting the energy surge through your body even more now feeling absolutely wonderful. On the next number that I count,

you will open your eyes, and you'll feel fantastic."

"Five, eyes open! Clear and alert!"

Emerging Difficult Subjects

Sometimes participants—particularly high school and college students in a stage show—will report feeling "out of it" after the experience.

Unfortunately, I know of several cases where hypnotists have just passed this off, like, "no big deal", or have said, "you must be on drugs, it's not my problem!" I have also seen hypnotists actually demand that these people go to the hospital. There is even one case where a hypnotist actually went in the ambulance with a participant who claimed she was "stuck in hypnosis..."

There are several factors that can cause this

1) The person is overly tired
2) The person is stressed, overwhelmed or emotional
3) The person is under the influence of drugs or alcohol (in which case they

should not have been hypnotized in the first place)

4) The person is confused
5) The person is "putting on a show," and their behavior is reinforced by their friends and family telling them that they are acting "weird."

I remember one stage show at a post-prom party. Many high schools have either post-prom or post-grad parties, organized as a "lock-in." All the kids are kept in a sports center or similar facility for the night after a prom or graduation to promote safety. I usually perform about 30 to 40 of these types of shows between the months of April and June.

Anyway, it was one of those shows. It was 4:30 in the morning, and I was exhausted and ready to go home. After the show, a group of people carried in one of the participants that was in my show just moments before. They were literally carrying him in as if he couldn't walk. They told me, "Something is wrong with Joey; fix him, something is wrong with him!"

After taking one look at Joey, it quickly became apparent that he was just putting on a show for everyone. He looked up at me with a silly smile on his face and said, "I feel special..."

I looked down at Joey, and I got down to his level and whispered in his ear, "We can do this the hard way, or the easy way. It's 4:30 in the morning, and I want to go home. If you make me do this the hard way, you're just going to end up embarrassing yourself in front of all your friends. He looked up at me with that same stupid silly grin and said, "I don't know what you're talking about." (Meanwhile, one of his friends was telling me that Joey can be quite dramatic at times and likes to call attention to himself.) This was all that I needed to hear. So, I looked down at Joey, and I said:

"Joey, close your eyes and listen to what I say. It's a great sign of intelligence to be hypnotized, which you displayed very well. You must be a pretty intelligent person. However, it's a greater sign of intelligence to come out of hypnosis when I count to five. I already did that once, and you were not able to come out of it as an intelligent person would. So, this time on my count of five, you're going to be wide-awake and back to normal, and if you're not, then all of your friends are going to see your true intelligence level... ONE, TWO..."

Before I could even get to the number three, he opened up his eyes and bounced up and said, "I'm fine. I'm fine. I really am smart, I promise!"

I looked at him and said, "I'm sure you are. Great job in the show and great job after the show." I winked at him, and we went our separate ways.

Creative Ways To Emerge A Difficult Subject

It will become apparent as to why a person may be difficult to emerge. You can use any of the techniques I will describe below, as they should cover all of the five categories mentioned above that could potentially cause a person to be difficult to emerge from hypnosis.

The Intelligence Method

This is the exact method I just mentioned above. This is a good method to use if you think somebody is putting on a show for their friends or family. This is also good to use if people misunderstood you or are not responding to your direct suggestions. A person wants to feel intelligent, and this method is a double bind they cannot refuse. I will also usually use this method if there is a group of people standing around the person.

A Stronger Emerging Method

Sometimes, people just need a method that is a little more direct. If a person comes up to me after the show claiming to feel strange, or if they did not emerge on my first attempt, I will use a stronger awakening technique. It goes a little something like this:

"On my count of five, you will open your eyes and be fully clear and alert. Nod your head if you understand." (Wait for a response.)

"With every number that I count, you will repeat that number. With every number I count, and with every number you count, you'll awaken more and more until we reach the number five. Nod your head if you understand."

"When you open your eyes, you will feel absolutely fantastic in every way. Nod your head if you understand..."

At this point, begin the count and make sure they are repeating after you.

CHAPTER 12

Rapid Re-inductions

If you know other methods to hypnotize people, and you don't feel really comfortable doing rapid inductions just *yet*, here is an easy way that will build both your confidence and your competence.

Hypnotize a client using your preferred method. While they are in hypnosis, condition them to go into hypnosis using a rapid method as a re-induction. That is when they are in hypnosis after you do whatever change work needs to be done, before you emerge them, build in a little trigger.

Here is some wording...

"The next time you come in this office, you'll easily be able to enter back into hypnosis with a simple shake of the hand."

"Allow your mind to record exactly how relaxed you are right now in this beautiful receptive state. In a moment, I will have you open your eyes."

"When your eyes are open, I will shake your hand and say "sleep.""

"As I do, just let your eyes close, and go into the same state you're in right now."

Repeat this with the client about four or five times to make sure the trigger is well reinforced, of course, deepening the state each time you practice. Then in the next session, all you have to do is have them look at you while you shake their hand and say, "sleep!"

You can build in any trigger you want here; simply use reinforcement and repetition to build the conditioning into the individual.

Building Your Confidence with The Rapid Induction Formula

One of the common questions I get asked is, "How do I make sure this is going to work in front of a group of people?" Remember the monkey see, monkey do induction? Utilize that process to your advantage. One of the easiest ways to begin using the Rapid Induction Formula is to cheat... Find out who in your group has been hypnotized before. Explain how, when a person is hypnotized once, it's easier for them to be hypnotized or re-enter hypnosis instantly. From there, proceed with the sleep talk and the sleep trigger.

Many of my good friends who are stage hypnotists will start off the show finding people who have been hypnotized before. The hypnotist will demonstrate on this person and use them as an example of how easily one can go into hypnosis, what it's like and how quickly it can happen.

CHAPTER 13

Your Questions Answered!

*I asked my friends and colleagues what they'd like to see in this book, or if they had questions they wished were answered somewhere. This chapter is based on their feedback and questions. Not only do you get **me**, but you get the added bonus of all my hypno-friends!*

Safety Concerns

Most hypnotists have heard of an induction called the "Arm Pull" induction. To an observer, it looks like a *slight* tug of the subject's arm, matched with a "sleep" command, causes a person to collapse into hypnosis. This leads some people to the misconception that, "Oh, the harder I pull their arm, the deeper into hypnosis they will go!" I have seen several stage hypnotists doing some variation of this induction, and they are pulling the participant's arm as if they are pulling it out of its socket!

If the thought crosses your mind that pulling harder is a good idea—please delete it. It's not true.

Here is how you achieve this same effect without causing bodily harm or injury to your subjects: **it's all in the wording.**

Paint the picture of how you want your subjects to respond. As long as you have built enough rapport with them, and have gained their compliance, then you will get the reaction you describe—without yanking on their arm.

It can sound something like this:

"When I touch your hand or gently push your hand down, your eyes will instantly close, and your entire body will relax and collapse into your chair as if you were a ragdoll or as if your body was heavy as a bag of wet sand."

At that point, gently give their hand a slight tug, and because of the instructions you have given the subject, they will react in a more dramatic fashion, and it will look like you are forcefully pushing their arm down, but you're really being quite gentle. You can use variations, such as "when I shake your hand" or "when I gently pull your arm," matching your action to the instruction.

You see, it's all in the language that you use. You want to be very descriptive in your instructions, artfully conveying how you want your subject to respond.

Safety With Standing Inductions

Just like an "arm pull," standing inductions can be fascinating to laypeople. However, you must keep in mind the safety of the subject.

I have seen hypnotists stand in front of a subject, place their hand on the back of the subject's neck, and then jerk the subject forward by the neck while shouting, "SLEEP!" This can be extremely dangerous for a person who has any neck or back injury—and if they don't, you don't want to cause one!

Avoid injury by, once again, crafting instructions with language that is gentler, but still results in a dramatic look. Saying something like:

Dan Candell's Rapid Induction Formula

"Close your eyes, and as I rock you back and forth, you allow yourself to relax, and

when I say sleep, your legs are strong beneath you and can support you, and you'll just lean your body on my shoulder."

This can be done in a very gentle way.

Also, be careful to ensure that you have their permission to "pop their personal bubble," so to speak, because this kind of induction requires that you get very close to your subject.

In another style of standing rapid induction, the subject starts in a standing position, and then you hypnotize them and lay them on the floor. There are a lot of debates about this style of induction: Is it right to lay someone on the floor? Is it just a power trip? Does the subject like this better?

I'll leave it to your own discretion to decide if this is something you want to do, or not. If you do choose to laypeople on the floor, you must consider several things:

1) Is the floor clean?

2) Is the subject wearing appropriate clothing for this? (Dresses, heels, skirts, etc., can cause many safety

issues or embarrassment for the subject.)

3) Do they want to be hypnotized in this style?

4) Is the situation congruent for this style of induction?

5) Are you physically able to handle a person flying into your arms?

In considering any type of standing induction, make sure that you can catch and gently lay a person down, if necessary, whether planned or not. Make sure you assume the appropriate stance. You do not want your feet to be together, instead, want to make sure you have your feet spread apart with one foot in front of you and one foot behind you, with the back leg slightly bent. In this position, you can handle a lot of weight coming at you. But, know your limits. The last thing you want is to be thrown off balance, or worse... have both you and your subject collapsing to the ground!

You need to **practice** catching people and laying them down gently, before doing standing inductions.

Dan Candell's Rapid Induction Formula

What If The Induction You Are Doing Fails?

One of the biggest fears—and why many hypnotists avoid instant and rapid inductions—is that the induction will fail. Guess what? Sometimes it does. If it does fail, it just means that induction wasn't right for the client, just like any other induction process.

Let's take a moment to reframe this, shall we?

Imagine doing a long, drawn-out progressive relaxation induction with a client in your office. You give the client great suggestions, and you finish the session. Upon emerging, the client says something like, "that was great, but I don't think I was hypnotized, and I don't think it worked." Or even this situation: you are part way through an induction, and the client opens their eyes and says, "I'm sorry, I don't think this is working!" What do you do? You simply move onto something else, or you switch it up the next time.

NOTE: Wouldn't you rather know right away if something didn't work? Or would you want to eat up all your time and your client's time before you realize something isn't working?

Remember, in the Rapid Induction Formula's **pre-frame**, you set the expectation, "I do rapid hypnosis, so we get results a lot faster." However, if it didn't work, you tell the client that rapid methods don't work for everyone, so let's do something that takes three minutes instead of three seconds. Guess what? You're still doing a rapid induction, but to the client, you're taking as long as it takes. Also, you can let the client know that there are many methods to hypnotize, and you start with the easiest and fastest methods first that work for most of the people most of the time.

What Follows Rapid Inductions?

Earlier, I discussed **why** I like and use rapid inductions, but you may be wondering if I would use them in all situations, or if the inductions ever change.

Rapid inductions are good for demonstrations, parties, street-style hypnosis, stage shows, and office clients. Can they change depending on the situation? Sure. One strength of the Rapid Induction Formula is that as a *formula*, you can vary the ingredients and still get good results. Usually, it's the purpose that will change the outcome.

If you are using rapid inductions for a performance setting such as a demonstration, a

Dan Candell's Rapid Induction Formula

show, or at a party, or on the street (more of a comical use), you will lead into a brief deepener and then pace for further instructions. For this purpose, the wording might be like this:

"In this state, you're still aware, but you are relaxed, and when you're in this state, you can follow my instructions easily, and everything I tell you will become so vivid as if it's real. It's almost as if my suggestions become your reality."

An office setting is nearly identical. After a deepener, you would proceed with giving the therapeutic suggestions and messages.

However, if it is more demonstrational or on the street, condition the participants even further by suggesting a further "sleep" trigger. The wording is something like:

"You'll continue to follow my instructions even when your eyes are open. Whenever I say the word 'SLEEP' or touch you on the forehead and say 'Sleep,' you will instantly allow your body to relax and collapse even deeper each time."

At this time, you don't have to do stage hypnosis skits; you can do basic challenges such as an eye-lock,[6] an arm catalepsy, or even a hand-stick.[7] Each time you have them do any type of suggestion or demonstration, it's using fractionation[8] to cause deeper and deeper hypnotic trance.

NOTE: Even though these routines are simple and basic to professional hypnotists, they are very intriguing to laypeople—the audience around you.

Give Back What You Took Away Or Strengthen Positive Suggestions!

After any type of hypnotic demonstration, always remember, when you emerge the subject, give them back what you took away, and take away any triggers you gave them during the demo. For example, if you did any type of name amnesia or sleep triggers, you want to make sure to remove those suggestions. Of course, if you've included suggestions at their request for self-improvement, those would be an exception.

---

[6] Also known as eye catalepsy, or eyelid catalepsy.
[7] In a hand-stick, you stick the subject's hand to a table, a surface, or even to themselves or their friend!
[8] Fractionation is the process of emerging and re-hypnotizing the subject, in order to deepen the hypnotic trance.

NOTE: I was doing a corporate demonstration in Orlando, Florida. I hypnotized about 12 people on stage in front of a group of 120 sales professionals. One of the routines I did was name amnesia. This is when you instruct the hypnotized participant that they will forget their name when you ask them. It is a classic amongst stage hypnotists, but it's a killer routine! However, at the end of that demo, I forgot to give them their names back. About an hour later, some people still had difficulty remembering their names. Because I was still there, I removed that suggestion for everyone. However, if I left and flew back home, would that suggestion stick with them? No. Eventually, they would realize that their name is important, and they need to remember it, and the suggestion would just wear off.

How Do I Practice The RIF?

I get a lot of phone calls asking if in my classes I provide people to practice with. Sometimes I can, and sometimes I can't. However, just like any skill, practice is essential.

The first step is getting the wording down and the timing. You may find practicing in front of a mirror or using your mobile device or camcorder to record yourself is a helpful method.

Once you have that down, start talking to people about how you do rapid hypnosis. This is the type of thing where you have to find the opportunity. Put yourself out there. Any time that you go out to restaurants, parties, the local shopping mall, or anywhere where there is a group of people. Any of these may be an opportunity to practice your skill.

Many communities have clubs or "meet-ups" that are open to people wanting to practice public speaking or amateur entertainment. Some of those groups would welcome something as unusual as a Rapid Induction Formula demonstration.

Remember, though, just like in all hypnosis, the participant needs to be willing—but you do not need a quiet atmosphere or a private place.

Let me tell you a story. At a restaurant, a friend and I were sitting at the bar, finishing dinner when a couple of women started talking to us. They told us that they were in town for a business conference. Somewhere in the conversation, it came up that I was a hypnotist. They both were very intrigued and expressed an interest in being hypnotized.

Dan Candell's Rapid Induction Formula

I used the RIF pre-frame to set the stage. Although it was noisy with people talking, plates and glasses clanking, and music playing, none of that mattered. I got her buy-in and had her do the finger magnets. The first time her fingers touched, I said, "Great! Keep looking at your fingers. Now, the next time you take your fingers apart, they will touch faster the second time, and when they touch, I will gently push your hands down and say 'sleep!' When I do, your eyes will close, and your body will instantly collapse into the chair, but I'll support you."

That was it! It worked wonders. I followed that with an arm catalepsy. By this time, we were attracting quite the crowd. After the arm catalepsy, I did name amnesia. When I was about to emerge her, her friend asked if I could do one more thing. She said, "My friend likes this guy, and I know he likes her too, but she's too afraid to call him and tell him how she feels. Can you do something about that?" I agreed, as long as her friend was okay with it.

I said to the hypnotized girl, "Is it okay with you if I give you superpower confidence to call this guy?" Without skipping a beat, she nodded her head in agreement. I said, "OK, Jen, on my count of five, you'll feel great. You'll remember your name, and you'll be back to normal in every way. One thing will be a little different, though. On my count of five, you will have extreme confidence as if it were a magical superpower. You'll feel fantastic, and you can do whatever you need or want to do with this new confidence."

Notice that I didn't tell her to go and call this guy, because the last thing I need is for her to feel like I *made* her call him. I counted her out of hypnosis, and it looked like a spark had been ignited in her. She said that she has never felt so good. After that, she and her friend went outside and called the gentleman. When she came back in, she had a smile that stretched from ear to ear. She had set up a date for when she returned back home, and the gentleman said that he felt the same way that she felt. A few months later, I got an email from her thanking me for the experience.

Dan Candell's Rapid Induction Formula

NOTE: When I was 12 years old and just learning hypnosis, I would line up all of my stuffed animals and pretend to hypnotize them. I would imagine they were *real* people. This boosted my confidence, flow, and wording. If I could do it for my *stuffed animal friends,* I could do it for a living, breathing people!

Tee- Shirts

When in doubt, get a tee-shirt made. The best way to practice is to get field experience and bring it to the streets. Several of my colleagues, myself included, have shirts that say something like, "Professional hypnotist, I hypnotize people fast!" Or "Ask me to hypnotize you quickly! I'm a professional hypnotist!" That sets the frame, and now, you have people coming up to YOU requesting to be hypnotized.

NOTE: If you are performing or practicing in public or on the streets, make sure you check your local laws. Some cities require special permits to do any type of public demonstration. At a hypnosis convention in Las Vegas, several of my colleagues went out on to infamous Freemont Street and started hypnotizing people. Soon after, the police came and cautioned the hypnotists that they can leave willingly or leave in handcuffs... this is a double-bind that you don't want to find yourself in!

CHAPTER 14

Now You Know!

Now you know how to hypnotize people quickly and confidently. You understand that rapid inductions do not have to be forceful or violent and that they can be more beneficial for both you and the client.

The next step is for you to **practice**. Find some friends or family members and practice going through the formula with them.

Keep in mind that family and friends are the most difficult people to hypnotize because, to them, you are *just* you—which isn't a bad thing. To them, you are not "The Hypnotist." When you practice on them, understand that you may just be going through the motions, but this will help you get good at the flow. Then, you can take it to the streets, parties, and even shows and clients.

These inductions can be done on groups of people and on individuals. Get the formula down, and you can plug and play to create a wide variety of different inductions and induction styles.

It was a pleasure teaching this method to you. Use it, practice it, get good at doing it. And the next time you see me, perhaps you can zap me into hypnosis by using my own formula.

As always, be well, do good and be true to who you are!

Happy Hypnotizing,
Dan Candell

About Dan's Mini-Course

Dan has a free companion course that goes with this book. It is free and can be found at:

www.RapidInductionFormula.com/Resources

This mini-course has videos and some additional resources you can check out.

Dan also teaches stage hypnosis and clinical hypnosis. He has several online courses and programs as well. You can find out more about all of his offerings at:

www.DanCandell.com

HAPPY HYPNOTIZING!

ABOUT THE AUTHOR

Dan Candell is a Certified Hypnosis Instructor and a Multi-Award-Winning Board-Certified Hypnotist. He travels around the world, teaching people how to positively program their subconscious minds to get more of what they want in life. He is also a stage hypnotist and has a very successful clinical practice and works with people from around the globe. He is known as "The Anxiety Relief Guy," and creator of The Anxiety Relief Revolution and the Break Free System. He uses Rapid Transformation Techniques to help people achieve the best version of themselves and to break free from anxiety and obstacles.

Printed in Great Britain
by Amazon